posh® creations

Color
BY
Number

Steve Duffendack

Andrews McMeel
PUBLISHING®

Posh® Creations

Andrews McMeel Publishing
a division of Andrews McMeel Universal
1130 Walnut Street, Kansas City, Missouri 64106

www.andrewsmcmeel.com

19 20 21 22 23 RLP 10 9 8 7 6 5 4 3 2 1

ISBN: 978-1-5248-5007-4

Editor: Patty Rice
Designer/Art Director: Julie Barnes
Production Editor: Julie Railsback
Production Manager: Tamara Haus

ATTENTION: SCHOOLS AND BUSINESSES
Andrews McMeel books are available at quantity discounts with
bulk purchase for educational, business, or sales promotional use.
For information, please e-mail the Andrews McMeel Publishing
Special Sales Department: specialsales@amuniversal.com.

Preface & Directions

When I began exploring the idea of a color by number book,
I immediately searched for a theme that could inspire and fill both
creative interests and the heart. I realized that for me, there is no better theme
than to focus on our earth's beautiful creations—all things natural. Thus the title
Posh Creations: Color By Number. The book explores animals, birds,
sea life, insects, plants, nature, and landscape themes. Just as the
title suggests the earth's creations, each page is also a creation
in and of itself as you, the colorist, fills in the outlines using the color key
at the bottom of the page to carefully reveal the final image. The book lays out
these precious subjects while winding through the four seasons of the year.

The color code on each page is simply a guide,
however, feel free to use your own creativity. There is a color key
in the back of the book, so you can choose to look ahead
and decide if you would prefer a different color palette.

I hope you as active participant find as much pleasure slowly coloring
and revealing each scene as I did creating them. Each page is filled
with thoughtfully engineered paths, sending you throughout the scene to build
step-by-step an exciting and graphically pleasing piece of art.
The pages are perforated for easy removal before you begin. Now all you need
are your favorite coloring supplies to join me in this unique process
of revelation and discovery.

Non-stop thanks go to my family—my wife, Alise, and our two greatest creations,
Spencer and Annalisa. They give me focus, strength, and joy!

Special thanks to my publisher Andrews McMeel Publishing, and my incredible
editor Patty Rice for the greatest support and partnership anyone could ask for.
Without you, my creations would never be revealed.

Happy coloring,

9

11

1 2 3 4 5 6 7 8

13

16

18

19

22

28

35

37

41

42

43

45

46

48

54

1 2 3 4 5 6 7 8 9 10

56

57

Color BY Number
• • • SOLUTIONS • • •

1

2

3

4

23

24

25

26

27

28

29

30

31

Steve Duffendack

Born and raised in Kansas City, Missouri, Steve has made
a career as an illustrator and designer for over 25 years.
Inspired by a lifelong passion for drawing and being creative,
Steve earned a BFA in graphic design with an emphasis in illustration
at the University of Missouri. While in school, Steve started his own
T-shirt design company while also providing editorial and political
cartoons for the school paper. After graduation, Steve taught
cartooning classes for kids and began a ten-year career at Hallmark Cards,
where he provided illustrations for gift bags, events, and home products.
For the next ten years, Steve worked as senior illustrator/designer for
a marketing company creating activity books, toys, cups, and crayons
for kids, all of which sparked his love for games, puzzles, and dot-to-dots.
Now as a freelance artist Steve has illustrated several coloring books
for adults, and is the creator for Andrews McMeel Syndication's feature,
Color Me Posh. Steve's work with Andrews McMeel Publishing can also
be found on the Posh Coloring Studio site.

In many wonderful ways, Steve's entire life
has lead to the creation of this book.
With a style that is both new and reminiscent,
Steve's whimsical approach and positive
outlook fill this collection with boundless joy.